LIVING IN NORTH & SOUTH AMERICA

Living in
THE USA

Jen Green

W
FRANKLIN WATTS
LONDON • SYDNEY

Franklin Watts
Published in paperback in Great Britain in 2019 by The Watts Publishing Group

Credits
Series Editor: Julia Bird
Editor: Sarah Silver
Series Design: D.R. ink

ISBN 978 1 4451 4873 1

Picture credits: Johnny Adolphson/Shutterstock: 12t. artzenter/Shutterstock: 15b. Atmosphere1/Shutterstock: 21b. Audiolui/Dreamstime: 19t. Blend Images/Alamy: 15t. Samuel Borges Photography/Shutterstock: 8t. Nicholas Burningham/Dreamstime: 6b. Ian Dagnall Computing/Alamy: 7t. Songquan Deng/Dreamstime: 9b. Songquan Deng/Shutterstock: 11t. Design Pics Inc/Alamy: 17t. East Village Images/Shutterstock: 13t. Gemenacom/Dreamstime: 17b. Juneisy Q. Hawkins/Shutterstock: 9t. Kenshi991/Shutterstock: 19c. Grzegorz Kielbasa/Dreamstime: 5b. Paul Langereis/Shutterstock: 18b. Susan Leggett/Dreamstime: 16b. Tanya Little/Shutterstock: 18t. MN Studio/Shutterstock: 20t. Monkey Business Images/Dreamstime: 7b. Monkey Business Images/Shutterstock: 6t, 10t. Luciana Mortula/Shutterstock: front cover. Rodney Murray/Shutterstock: 5t. Josef Pittner/Shutterstock: 13b. Sandbox Studio/Shutterstock: 12b. Gina Sanders/Dreamtime: 8b. Olga Sapegina/Shutterstock: 4t. Tinnaporn Sathapornnanont/Dreamtime: 10b, 23t. Seagull_L/Shutterstock: 14b. Sipa Press/Rex Shutterstock: 11b. Alena Sivyi/Dreamstime: 19b. Kenneth Sponsler/Dreamstime: 20b. Spotmatik Ltd/Shutterstock: 16t. 3445128471/Shutterstock: 14t. Zuma Press/Alamy: 21t.

Printed in Dubai

Franklin Watts
An imprint of
Hachette Children's Group
Part of The Watts Publishing Group
Carmelite House
50 Victoria Embankment
London EC4Y 0DZ

An Hachette UK Company
www.hachette.co.uk

www.franklinwatts.co.uk

Contents

Welcome to the USA   4

People in the USA   6

New York and Washington   8

Cities   10

Scenery and wildlife   12

What we eat   14

Having fun   16

Amazing places   18

Festivals and holidays   20

USA: Fast facts   22

Glossary   23

Index   24

Words in bold are in the glossary on page 23.

Welcome to the USA

Hi! I live in the USA — the United States of America. My country is also called America or just the US.

HAWAII

ALASKA

CANADA

Pacific Ocean

SAN FRANCISCO

HAWAII

LOS ANGELES

Rocky Mountains

Missouri River

THE USA

CHICAGO

Appalachians

Mississippi River

NEW YORK

WASHINGTON D.C.

Atlantic Ocean

NEW ORLEANS

MEXICO

HOUSTON

Where is the USA?

The USA is a big country in North America. It shares **borders** with Canada and Mexico. It has two long **coastlines**, with the Pacific Ocean to the west, and the Atlantic to the east.

Fifty states

The USA is made up of fifty states, plus the District of Columbia. Forty-eight states are joined together to form the main part of the country. Alaska, the biggest state, lies to the north west of Canada. The fiftieth state, Hawaii, lies out in the Pacific Ocean.

Mount Denali, in Alaska, is the highest mountain in the USA.

Weather

The USA is so big that different parts have different **climates**. Alaska in the far north is cool in summer, and freezing cold in winter. Southern states and Hawaii have a warm, wet climate. Coasts are generally milder than places far inland. Parts of the southwest are very dry.

Death Valley is the hottest, driest place in the USA.

People in the USA

I was born in the USA. My country has over 300 million people. The people of the USA are usually called Americans. Children are usually called kids!

Many peoples

Native Americans were the first people to live in what is now the USA. From the 1600s, Europeans, such as the English and the Spanish settled on the east coast. They slowly spread west across the country, taking the lands of the Native Americans. In the 1700s, black Africans were brought to the USA to work as **slaves**, but slavery ended in the 1860s.

A traditional Native American dance

Immigrants arriving in New York City from Europe in the early 20th century

New arrivals

In the 1800s and 1900s, people from many different nations came to the USA. These newcomers were called **immigrants**. They came from Ireland and other parts of Europe, from China and Central and South America. Each group brought their own **customs** and beliefs.

So many people have come to live in the **USA** that it is called a 'nation of immigrants'.

Religion

Religion is important to a lot of Americans. Most people are Christian – mainly **Protestant** or **Roman Catholic**. There are also many Jews and Muslims.

New York and Washington

*I live in New York City. It's the city with the most people in the USA, but not the **capital**. The capital is Washington, in the District of Columbia, known as Washington D.C..*

Crowded city

Over 8.6 million people live in New York City. The city started on Manhattan Island in the mouth of the Hudson and East Rivers. It grew quickly in the 1800s. Space was cramped on the island, so people built upwards, and the first **skyscrapers** appeared.

Skyscrapers rise above the streets of New York City.

The Statue of Liberty is on an island in New York City harbour. It stands 93 metres high.

Freedom statue

New York City's most famous **landmark** is the Statue of Liberty. This huge statue was a gift from the French people. It stands for freedom. Since the 1880s, this statue has welcomed immigrants arriving by boat.

The Capitol

Washington D.C.

Washington D.C. is the home of the US government. The **president** lives and works in the White House. The government, called Congress, meets in the Capitol. Washington has many monuments and statues of famous presidents and politicians.

Cities

Eight out of every ten
Americans live in cities.
I live in Los Angeles,
on the west coast.

West coast cities

Los Angeles is the USA's second-largest city. It is home to Hollywood, the American film industry. Films made in Hollywood are shown all over the world. To the north is the city of San Francisco, near a place where gold was discovered in the 1880s.

The famous Golden Gate Bridge is in San Francisco.

The Willis Tower in Chicago is one of the tallest buildings in the USA.

Chicago

Chicago lies on Lake Michigan, one of five Great Lakes, which lie close to the Canadian border. In the past these linked lakes were used to transport crops and **minerals**. But today most goods go by truck, train or plane.

New Orleans

New Orleans, in the south, lies near the mouth of the Mississippi River. The city is known for jazz music. In 2005, it was hit by a **hurricane,** which flattened houses and caused flooding. Since then, the city has been rebuilt.

Population of largest cities

New York City: 8.6 million
Los Angeles: 4 million
Chicago: 2.7 million
Houston: 2.2 million

Flooding in New Orleans in 2005

Scenery and wildlife

The USA is a vast country with all sorts of amazing scenery. There are mountains, plains and valleys, deserts, forests and beautiful beaches on the coast.

Mountains and plains

Two great mountain ranges run down western and eastern USA. The Rocky Mountains rise in the west, the Appalachians in the east. In between lie the Great Plains, the USA's main farmlands. Farmers grow wheat, corn and soya beans, and raise cattle and pigs.

growing wheat

geyser

Yellowstone
National Park

bison

National parks

National parks help protect some of America's most beautiful countryside. Yellowstone National Park in the Rockies was the world's first national park. It was set up in 1872. Here you can see craggy mountains, lakes and geysers that shoot jets of hot water into the air.

Caribou in Alaska

Wildlife

Each part of the USA has its own wildlife. Polar bears and caribou live in Alaska. Mountain goats, bison and grizzly bears roam the Rocky Mountains. Rattlesnakes and lizards thrive in southwestern deserts. Alligators and turtles lurk in swamps in the southeast.

What we eat

You can eat all kinds of delicious food in the USA. Our favourite food is pizza! This dish came from Italy.

Local foods

Each part of the USA has its own style of cooking. Seafood such as lobster is served on the coast. West-coast cities are known for Chinese cooking, while spicy Mexican foods are eaten in the southwest. French and Italian immigrants brought their own dishes, too.

Jambalaya is typical in Louisiana. It is influenced by French and Spanish food.

French fries

Fast food

The USA is the home of fast foods such as fried chicken, burgers and hot dogs. These are often served with French fries (chips) and washed down with a milkshake. American fast foods are popular all over the world.

lobster

$36.99/LB

Breakfast, lunch and dinner

Our family has toast, fruit or cereal for breakfast. Some people eat pancakes! At lunch many people have a sandwich. Dinner is often the main meal. There may be meat or fish with salad or vegetables. Sometimes we have pasta. Dessert may be ice cream, pie or cake.

Having fun

Americans are famous as hard workers. But when we're not working or studying, we like to have fun!

playing American football

Sport

Watching and playing sport are popular pastimes. Our favourite sports are baseball, basketball and American football. Golf and tennis are also popular – many golf and tennis champions come from the USA.

Outdoors ...

Outdoors, I love riding my bike, skateboarding and swimming. In the summer, we drive to the coast for surfing and sailing. Some people camp, hike or fish in the mountains in summer, and ski and snowboard there in winter. Closer to home, we head for the city centre to meet friends, shop, catch a movie or visit a museum or zoo.

A family camping in Alaska

... and indoors

Indoors, we play video games and find out about things on the Internet. I visit friends to watch movies, TV shows or listen to music. Nearly every American home has at least one TV and computer, and many kids have a computer in their room.

playing computer games

Amazing places

The USA has many awesome places to visit. People come from all over the world to see the sights.

Natural wonders

Yosemite is a beautiful national park in California. There are sheer rock faces, rugged mountains and waterfalls. A mountain called the Half Dome looks like it's been sliced in two! It's a great place to camp.

the Half Dome

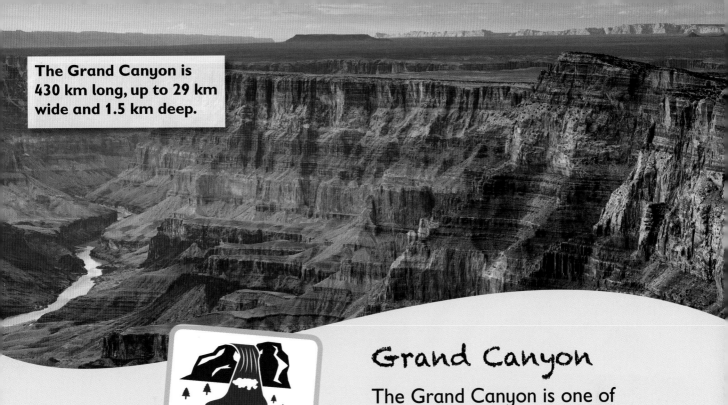

The Grand Canyon is 430 km long, up to 29 km wide and 1.5 km deep.

Grand Canyon

The Grand Canyon is one of the world's deepest and widest canyons. You have to be very careful near the edge! The sheer canyon walls plunge steeply to the Colorado River far below.

Waterfalls

Niagara Falls lies on the border with Canada. The river plunges 53 metres over a cliff, and spray fills the air.

Theme parks

Wherever you live, you won't be too far from a **theme park**. The most famous is Disneyland in California. It is based on the films of cartoonist Walt Disney. Many theme and water parks have thrilling rollercoasters, water splashes and slides.

a rollercoaster in North Carolina

Festivals and holidays

*Everyone loves a holiday! Some holidays are religious **festivals**. We also celebrate important dates in our history.*

Holy days

The biggest Christian festivals are Easter and Christmas. The festival of Mardi Gras marks **Lent**, the period before Easter. In New Orleans people parade through the streets in colourful costumes. Important Jewish festivals include Yom Kippur and Hanukkah – the festival of lights.

Christmas lights decorate a town in Ohio

Thanksgiving

At Thanksgiving, in November, we give thanks for the good things in life. Families gather to share a special meal, usually with turkey. This tradition remembers a feast held in 1621 by the first English settlers to celebrate the harvest.

A family celebrating Thanksgiving

A fireworks display for Independence Day in Los Angeles

Independence Day

Independence Day falls on 4 July. By the 1700s, English settlers had established thirteen **colonies** along the east coast, which were ruled by Britain. In 1775–83, the colonies fought a war against Britain and won independence. We celebrate with picnics and barbecues. There are parades and fireworks in towns and cities across the land.

USA: Fast facts

Capital: Washington D.C.

Population: 329 million (2018)

Area: 9.85 million square km

Languages: No official language. English is the main language spoken, followed by Spanish.

Currency: US dollar ($)

Main religions: Christianity, Judaism, Islam, Buddhism, Hinduism

Longest river: Missouri, 3,768 km

Highest mountain: Mt Denali, 6,190 m

National holidays: New Year's Day (1 January), Martin Luther King Jr. Day (third Monday in January), Washington's Birthday (third Monday in February), Easter, Memorial Day (last Monday in May), Independence Day (4 July), Labor Day (first Monday in September), Veterans Day (11 November), Thanksgiving (fourth Thursday in November), Christmas Day (25 December)

Glossary

border a line marking the boundary between two countries

capital city where the country's government meets

climate the regular weather pattern in a region

coastline where the land meets the sea

colony (pl. colonies) an area ruled by another country

custom a traditional way of doing things, that has been followed for many years

festival a celebration, usually for religious reasons

hurricane a huge, powerful storm with whirling winds

immigrant a person who comes to live permanently in a country that is not their own

landmark a very important building or place

Lent the forty days before Easter

minerals solid, non-living substances of which the Earth is made

national park a protected area of countryside that people can visit

president the leader of the USA

Protestant a branch of Christianity that doesn't have the Pope as its head

Roman Catholic a branch of Christianity that has the Pope as its head

skyscraper a very tall building

slave a person who is considered to be 'owned' by someone else and is forced to work for no pay

theme park a big, outdoor amusement park, with rides and other attractions

Index

A

Alaska 4, 5, 13, 17,
Appalacians 4, 12,

B

borders 4

C

Capitol 9
Chicago 4, 11
Christian 7, 20, 22
cities 8–9, 10–11, 17, 21
colonies 21
Congress 9

D

Death Valley 5
deserts 5, 12, 13

F

farming 12
festivals 20–21
food 14–15, 21

G

geyser 13
Golden Gate Bridge 10
Grand Canyon 19

H

Hawaii 4, 5
holidays 20–21, 22
Hollywood 10
Houston 4, 11
hurricane 11

I

immigrants 7, 9, 14
Independence Day 21, 22

L

lakes 11, 13
landscape 12–13, 17, 18, 19
Los Angeles 4, 10, 11, 21

M

Mexico 4
Mount Denali 5, 22
mountains 4, 5, 12, 13, 17, 18,
   22

N

Native Americans 6
New Orleans 4, 11, 20
New York City 4, 7, 8, 9, 11
Niagara Falls 19

P

population 6, 8, 11, 22
president 9

R

religion 7, 20, 22
rivers 4, 8, 11, 19, 22

S

San Francisco 4, 10
settlers 6, 21
skyscrapers 8
slaves 6
sports 16, 17
Statue of Liberty 9

T

Thanksgiving 21, 22
theme parks 19

W

Washington D.C. 4, 8, 9, 22
weather 5
White House 9
wildlife 13